Sam's Sister
Tenth Anniversary Edition

Written by Juliet C. Bond, LCSW
Illustrated by Linda Hoffman Kimball

Printed in the United States of America
Published by Marcinson Press, Jacksonville, Florida

For bulk purchases or to carry this book in your
bookstore, library, school, agency or retail establishment,
please contact the publisher at marcinsonpress.com.

ISBN 978-0-9967207-8-6

Published by Marcinson Press
10950-60 San Jose Blvd., Suite 136
Jacksonville, FL 32223 USA
http://www.marcinsonpress.com

Find us on Facebook!
http://www.facebook.com/samssisterbook

Sam's Sister

WRITTEN BY JULIET C. BOND, LCSW
ILLUSTRATED BY LINDA HOFFMAN KIMBALL

About the Author

Juliet C. Bond, LCSW is a social worker, mother, foster parent, and children's book writer from Evanston, IL. She wrote *Sam's Sister* while working with birth mothers who struggled to explain their open adoption plans to the children they were parenting. Over 60% of birth mothers are already parenting other children when they make an adoption plan. Hoping to provide an avenue for parents and children to deal with grief and loss issues related to adoption, she wrote this book. More than a decade later, the book has become a staple, used by adoption agencies and parents across the country. She hopes this re-release, with new illustrations, an affordable paperback format, and an important resource section will continue to bring comfort to families making such an important life decision.

About the Illustrator

Linda Hoffman Kimball illustrates for adults and for children in various media. Like the recurring lovey, Rosa's rooster, who is given to Sam at the end of the story, Linda's illustrations include a depth of humor and heart that work beautifully in a book like *Sam's Sister*. Her illustrations appear in books published by Houghton Mifflin, Ballantine, Norton, Children's Press, and in numerous magazines and periodicals. She earned a BA from Wellesley College and an MFA from Boston University. Check out her website at LindaHoffmanKimball.com.

**To Jacob, Mairita, Lilly,
Toms, Casey, Tomas,
and to mothers and children
everywhere
– birth or chosen –
as you navigate and enjoy
this colorful world.**

*"Y por eso los grandes amores de
muchos colores me gustan a mi."
And that is why the great love of
many colors is pleasing to me.
JCB*

*To the Polo Girls – thanks for the
music and the memories.
LHK*

Introduction

by Carrie Goldman

Author of "Bullied: What Every Parent, Teacher, and Kid Needs to Know About Ending the Cycle of Fear" and co-author of the "Jazzy's Quest" adoption series

The evolution of open adoption has revealed the hunger of birth families for resources that can help their children process the placement of siblings. In this anniversary re-release of *Sam's Sister*, an adoption classic gets a face-lift with new illustrations and an extensive list of resources for parents and children!

Though there are many children's picture books available to help adoptees process their feelings, there is only one book for the siblings of children placed for adoption. That book is *Sam's Sister*. It was one of the first books I read to my daughter, and it was one she asked for again and again.

In *Sam's Sister*, author Juliet Bond has created a masterful story that captures the trajectory of anxiety, grief, and ultimate acceptance of a five-year-old girl whose pregnant mother is making plans to place her new baby brother for adoption. Stories offer a powerful way for people to access their inner emotions, and *Sam's Sister* will strike a responsive chord with children who are struggling to articulate how they feel about having their siblings grow up in adoptive families.

Beautifully weaving song lyrics with poignant prose, Juliet Bond – both an adoption social worker and a foster mother – has provided us with a treasure. She captures the tremulous mixture of hope and sadness surrounding any adoption. Authentic in dialogue and sensitive to cultural differences between the birth and adoptive families, *Sam's Sister* is a must-have for birth and adoptive families.

When I was five, something
very special happened.

At first, I was worried. I asked Mommy, "Are you thinking hard about something? Why are you so quiet? Why aren't you smiling?"

"I was sure something was on her mind when I sang our favorite song, 'De Colores,' and Mommy said, "Stop being so loud, Rosa!"

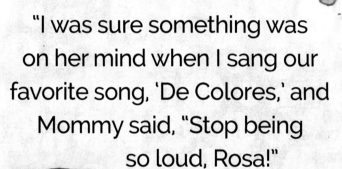

I was worried Mommy was sick. Maybe she didn't love me anymore.

"Mommy," I asked. "What's wrong?"

She sat me on her lap. "Rosa, Mommy has been very worried about something. You should know what it is."

She smiled, but her eyes looked sad.

"There is a new baby growing in my tummy, but when he's born, I can't take care of him." Mommy said. "We don't have enough room here. We don't have a crib or special baby food, or even a stroller to push the baby in."

"We can use my toy stroller!" I said.

"That wouldn't be safe, Rosa. And we'd need someone to watch the baby while I'm at work and you're at school."

"I'll help!"

Mommy shook her head. "No, Rosa. Babies need energy and lots of attention. Right now, I couldn't provide those things for *two* children, even with your help."

Mommy took a deep breath. "I might know what to do. I met a family who want a baby to love. They hope we will let them take care of the baby in my tummy."

"Will they take me, too?" I asked.

"No way, José!" she said, and hugged me tight. "We have just what we need to take care of each other and you will always live with me. I love you very, very much."

"Do you love the baby in your tummy?" I asked.

"Yes, we will love him, too. He just won't live with us."

Soon Mommy's tummy grew big.
I had lots of questions.

"Will I be the baby's sister?" I asked,
because sometimes I wanted the baby
to stay with us.

Mommy said, "Even though he won't
live here, you will always be the baby's
big sister, Rosa."

One day, we went to a restaurant to meet the baby's parents. "Do you have a stroller?" I blurted. The mama had a pretty smile. "Hi, Rosa." She said. "I'm Sara and this is Joe."

Joe had a deep, warm laugh like the rumble trucks make when they thunder up our street. "We've had a stroller waiting for a baby for a long time."

"And we brought you a present! This is a coloring book that doesn't have anything in it yet. Would you like to fill it with pictures for the baby?"

I nodded. I liked that I had a way to tell the baby that I love him, too.

On the night my brother was born, I had a sleepover at Auntie Maria's house. In the morning, she brought me to the hospital. Joe and Sarah were already there. Sarah took my hand, "Rosa, the baby's name is going to be Sam."

Joe's smile wrinkled the corners of his eyes. "We hope you and your mommy will pick out a middle name for Sam." He handed me a blue envelope. "This is a special letter from me and Sarah. You can read it when you get home."

In Mommy's hospital room, I met Sam.

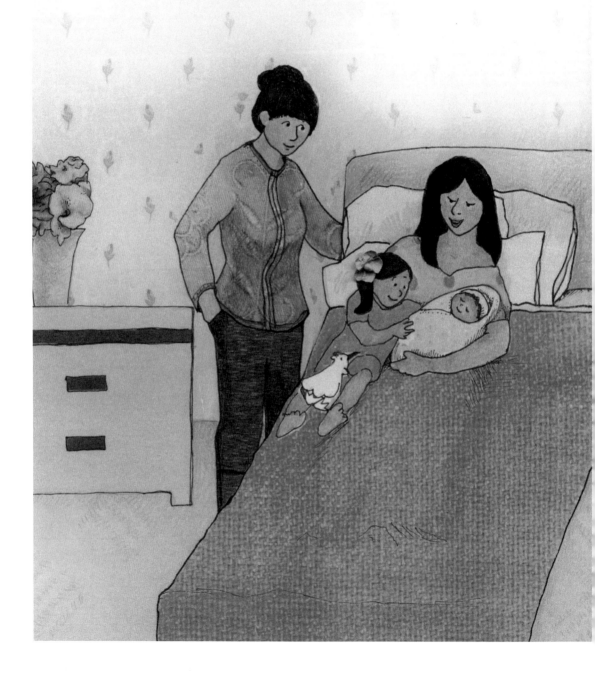

"Mommy, Mommy!" I called out, climbing onto the bed with her. "We get to pick a middle name for Sam!"

After trying out many names, we decided on *Querido* because it means *wanted* in Spanish.

"Sam should always know that he was wanted," said Mommy. "He was wanted by us and by Sarah and Joe."

That night, Mommy came home with me, and Sam went home with Sarah and Joe.

We waited until we were both tucked into Mommy's bed, and then we read the letter that promised to take such good care of Sam.

Dear Laura and Rosa,

We are overwhelmed by the trust that you have placed in us. Our long awaited dream of becoming parents has finally come true!

We know that this was not an easy decision for you and that you might sometimes feel very sad. We know that you suffered for our happiness. But never forget that you are the bearers of joy.

You will always be an important part of Sam's life. The power of Sam's growing life before birth, the reason for his freckles and crooked smile; these are things only you can tell him about.

We will always love and care for Sam. We will sing to him, read to him, stroll him through the park, and take him on vacations with our families. We will hold him when he skins his knees and dry his tears when he cries. He will be our world.

We will thank you every day for making us Sam's parents.

Love,
Sarah and Joe

We cried while we read the letter. Later that night, I had a nightmare and needed to sleep with Mommy in her bed.

"We are going to a special counselor to talk about how much we miss Sam," Mommy said. "Even though we know that Sam is happy with Sarah and Joe, sometimes we will still be sad that he doesn't live with us."

Right away Sarah and Joe sent pictures and videos. I liked the ones where Sam was smiling or chewing on a toy. They also called every Thursday night to tell us about the new things that Sam was doing.

Joe told us, "He laughs when we kiss him!"

Sarah said, "His favorite song is 'De Colores!'"

After that phone call, Mommy began singing again.

On the Saturday after kindergarten ended,
we visited Sam at Sarah and Joe's house.

"Sam is so big!" I said. "He can almost sit up."

I sang him "De Colores." He smiled and gurgled like he was singing, too. When I made silly faces, he reached for me.

Sam had a big crib just like Mommy said he would. But I didn't see a stroller. I asked Joe, "Where is Sam's stroller?"

Joe gave one of his big laughs. "You're a good sister to think about that."

In the garage, Joe showed me
Sam's big green stroller.

After our visit, I told Mommy, "I feel happy."
She took my hand and said, "Me too, Rosa."

Sometimes I miss Sam. Then I need to talk to Mommy or draw in my "Sam" coloring book. But I know Sam is where he should be.

And even though he doesn't live with Mommy and me, we will always be part of his family.

Because when I was five, something very special happened

I became Sam's Sister.

De Colores

De colores,
De colores se visten los campos
En la primavera

De colores,
De colores son los pajaritos
Que vienen de fuera

De colores,
De colores es el arcoiris
Que vemos lucir

Y por eso los grandes amores
De muchos colores
Me gustan a mi

Canta el gallo,
Canta el gallo con el
Quiri, quiri, quiri,
Quiri, quiri

La gallina,
La gallina con el
Cara, cara, cara,
Cara, cara

Los polluelos,
Los polluelos con el
Pio, pio, pio, pio

Y por eso los grandes amores
De muchos colores
Me gustan a mi

In Colors

In colors,
In colors the fields are dressed
In the springtime

In colors,
Colorful are the little birds
That come from far away

In colors,
Colorful is the rainbow
That we see shine

And that is why the great love
Of many colors
Is pleasing to me

Sings the rooster,
Sings the rooster with the
Cock-a-doodle-do,
Cock-a-doodle do

The hen,
The hen with the
Cluck, cluck, cluck,
Cluck, cluck.

The baby chicks,
The baby chicks with the
Peep, peep, peep, peep

And that is why the great love
Of many colors
Is pleasing to me

Author-Recommended Resources

What is Open Adoption?

Open adoption allows adoptive parents, birth parents, the adopted child, and any siblings to interact. Openness varies from family to family and often changes as children grow older.

Due to a growing recognition that there are benefits to allowing connections and communications across birth and adoptive families, open adoption has become progressively common.

How Can Parents Gain a Better Understanding of Open Adoption?

- Talk with professionals who handle adoption
- Meet with a counselor or therapist with knowledge and experience in open adoption
- Explore websites
- Read blogs that provide information and research as well as blogs that relay personal experiences
- Read articles and books about open adoption

Books for Parents

Adoption Nation: How the Adoption Revolution Is Transforming Our Families – and America by Adam Pertman

Adoption Parenting: Creating a Toolbox, Building Connections by Jean MacLeod and Sheena Macrae

Being Adopted: The Lifelong Search for Self by Brodzinsky, Schecter and Henig

In On It: What Adoptive Parents Would Like You to Know About Adoption. A Guide for Relatives and Friends by Elisabeth O'Toole

In Their Own Voices: Transracial Adoptees Tell Their Stories by Rita J. Simon and Rhonda M. Roorda

Websites for Parents

The Donaldson Adoption Institute
Empowered to Connect
Adoption.net
Adopting.org
Adoption Learning Partners

Websites for Kids

JazzysQuest.com

Fictional Picture Books for/about Young Children

A Mother for Choco by Keiko Kasza
Pink Baby Alligator by Judith A. Barrett
The Best Single Mom in The World by Mary Zisk
I Love You Like Crazy Cakes by Rose A. Lewis
And Tango Makes Three by Justin Richardson

Non-fiction Books for/about Younger Children

Maybe Days: A Book for Children in Foster Care
    by Jennifer Wilgocki
My New Family: A First Look at Adoption by Pat Thomas
Let's Talk About Adoption by Fred Rogers
A Forever Family by Boslyn Banish
All About Adoption: How Families are Made and How Kids Feel About It by Marc A. Nemiroff and Jane Anunziata

Chapter Books for Children

The *Jazzy's Quest* series by Juliet Bond & Carrie Goldman
Returnable Girl by Pamela Lowell
See No Color by Shannon Gibney
Find a Stranger Say Goodbye by Lois Lowry
Breadcrumbs by Anne Ursu

If you enjoyed this book, make your voice heard.

Want to see more books like
Sam's Sister – books about adoption,
dealing with difficult situations, diversity,
acceptance, and inclusion?

You can make it happen!

We would greatly appreciate your
taking a quick minute or two to write
an online review for this book. Online
reviews are an extremely important tool
for readers, authors, libraries, schools,
and bookstores to spread the word and
increase the popularity of diverse books
for children. Every review counts.

Thanks and happy reading!

Find *Sam's Sister* on Facebook:
facebook.com/samssisterbook

MARCINSON PRESS

Made in the USA
Las Vegas, NV
11 February 2024

85646582R00026